THE LATER YEARS OF BRITISH RAILWAYS 1980–1995

Volume Two – Eastern and Southern England

Patrick Bennett

AMBERLEY

First published 2018

Amberley Publishing
The Hill, Stroud
Gloucestershire, GL5 4EP

www.amberley-books.com

Copyright © Patrick Bennett, 2018

The right of Patrick Bennett to be identified as
the Author of this work has been asserted in
accordance with the Copyrights, Designs and
Patents Act 1988.

ISBN 978 1 4456 7518 3 (print)
ISBN 978 1 4456 7519 0 (ebook)

British Library Cataloguing in Publication Data.
A catalogue record for this book is available from
the British Library.

Origination by Amberley Publishing.

Contents

Introduction

In 1980, the area that this book covers had been little affected by change since the days of steam. Intercity trains were almost all hauled by diesel locomotives, while local trains were in the hands of first-generation diesel multiple units. There was considerable freight traffic, much of it still carried in short-wheelbase wagons. Marshalling yards, such as March, were still active and busy. On the Southern Region, most services were still provided using slam-door electric or diesel-electric multiple units based on the Mk 1 body shell. In much of the East Midlands and in East Anglia, traditional signalling was still the norm. Through the following fifteen years the changes that took place made the railways of 1980 seem almost unrecognisable.

On the Great Northern route, the much-loved Deltic locomotives gave way to the HST, which in turn gave way to electric trains once the electrification through to Leeds and Edinburgh was completed in 1991. In 1987 electrification reached Cambridge and was extended to King's Lynn in 1992. The Great Eastern Main Line was electrified through to Norwich by 1986 and the Midland Main Line was electrified between St Pancras and Bedford in 1983. Meanwhile, from the early 1980s onwards, new diesel multiple units started to be introduced, displacing first-generation types. Freight traffic went into a rapid decline and some traffics, such as newspapers and parcels, were lost altogether. The run-down of the coal industry had a severe impact in the East Midlands. On the organisational side there were many changes; not least among these was the setting up of Network South East in 1982, as well as the introduction of sectorisation in the same period. Finally, privatisation arrived in the mid-1990s, and with it the exploding of the railway into a thousand fragments.

When compiling this book, twenty-two years after the last photograph was taken, what struck me very forcibly was that in this latter period the railway has changed to an even greater extent than in the preceding fifteen years. The passenger railway is now almost entirely in the hands of multiple units of various kinds. Freight has declined catastrophically, not least because of the closing down of the British mining industry. Many freight-only lines have closed, and whole swathes of freight infrastructure – sidings, terminals and marshalling yards – have been swept way. Traditional signalling is becoming an endangered species, with huge areas now being controlled by single centres. The result of all this change is that the vast majority of images in this book depict scenes that have gone forever. They are, in that sense, historical.

In putting together this work I have tried to include as broad a sweep as possible of the railway that existed in the final years of BR and I hope others will enjoy reading this book as much as I have enjoyed writing it. The author and publisher would like to thank the following people for permission to use copyright material in this book: Peter Groom for the photographs taken at March and Temple Mills; Chris Gwilliam for the photographs taken at Nottingham and Coalville; Ben Brooksbank for the photographs taken at London Bridge, Temple Mills and Stratford; Lamberhurst for the photograph taken at Hastings; and Martin Addison for the photographs taken at Wembley and Willesden.

Millay, France
September 2017

East Anglia

Cambridge to King's Lynn

The line from London to Cambridge was started by the Grand Northern & Eastern Railway (originally of 5-foot gauge) and was completed by the Eastern Counties Railway (ECR), opening in 1845. The ECR was reluctant to extend its line northwards, its target being Norwich, and it fell to the East Anglian Railway (EAR) to complete the line to King's Lynn, which was opened in 1847. On 21 August 1980 a Class 105 Cravens unit waits to leave Cambridge with the 09.50 service to Ipswich.

No. 31269 is at Ely, waiting to leave with the 11.30 King's Lynn to Liverpool Street on 30 August 1980. In the days before electrification, the Class 31s together with the Class 37s were the mainstay of the London–King's Lynn route.

By 1989, much has changed. 'Skinhead' No. 31134 approaches Ely hauling a Network South East-liveried rake of Mk 2 coaches, forming the 15.28 King's Lynn–Cambridge. 13 September 1989.

Electrification reached Cambridge in 1987 and King's Lynn in 1992. In early 1992 there was a blockade of Ely in order to carry out resignalling. A temporary station was built at Chettisham. The original station closed in 1960; the station building can be seen on the left. On 15 April 1992 a Class 156 DMU arrives to pick up passengers. Chettisham signal box has since been abolished.

King's Lynn station as seen from the country end. A Class 47 waits to leave with a train for London.

King's Lynn Junction signal box. This box controls the junction with the line to Middleton Towers. This line, built by the Lynn & Dereham Railway in 1848, originally extended to Dereham. It closed entirely in 1968, except for the section to Middleton Towers, which was retained in order to service the sand quarries at that location. 17 April 1990.

No. 58040 *Cottam Power Station* runs its train under the sand hopper at Middleton Towers station.

The loaded train (6E83) stands in the yard, waiting to depart for Monk Bretton. 12 April 1995

Fifteen years earlier we see the same train with a different engine but with the same wagons. This is No. 37171 on 30 August 1980.

King's Lynn was once connected to lines to Hunstanton and Wells, Dereham and the Midland & Great Northern (M&GN) network, as well as to the Cambridge line. At South Lynn were the exchange sidings with the M&GN; here we see contractors lifting these sidings, one of the last vestiges of the M&GN, on 12 April 1995.

Between King's Lynn and Ely lies Downham Market. Its elegant station is a listed building.

Unit No. 317342 passes the King's Lynn Harbour branch as it departs southwards. The line on the left led to the harbour, while that on the right was an industrial siding. Both have now been lifted and plain line substituted.

March

The line from March to Peterborough was built by the ECR and opened in 1847. The Wisbech line was opened by the Wisbech, St Ives & Cambridge Junction Railway, also in 1847, shortly after which it was absorbed into the ECR. After a long battle over who should build the line from March to Spalding, the Great Northern Railway (GNR) and the Great Eastern Railway (GER), successor to the ECR, agreed to set up a joint committee and the line opened in 1867. The line south to St Ives/Huntingdon, built earlier by the EAR and ECR, also came under the Great Northern & Great Eastern Joint Committee (GN&GEJt). The March–Spalding line closed as recently as October 1982. No. 60080 passes March East signal box with an Ely–Peak Forest working. The GER type 5 signal box was built by Saxby & Farmer in 1885 and it is now a listed building. 12 April 1995.

Much earlier, Class B17 'Sandringham' No. 61642 *Kilverstone Hall* heads off in the opposite direction with a train for Ely. 26 August 1958. (Photograph: Peter Groom)

Above and below: Whitemoor Marshalling Yard was once the largest in Britain. It closed in May 1984, following which it was used for storing redundant locomotives. March MPD closed in 1992. Subsequently, part of the yard has been reopened by Network Rail, and GB Railfreight have established a depot there. 18 April 1990.

No. 56101 is seen on 12 April 1995 at Waldersea level crossing on the Wisbech–March line. The train is 6S93, the Wisbech–Deanside Nestlé Purina pet food train. Passenger services were withdrawn in 1968 and the last freight train ran in 2000. Track remains in place and a number of plans to reopen the line have been put forward but none have gotten much further than the discussion stage. It is reported that Network Rail have quoted a sum of £100 million to bring the line back to passenger status.

Cambridge and Bury St Edmunds Line

The line from Cambridge to Bury St Edmunds and beyond had a curious beginning. The Newmarket & Chesterford Railway built a line from Chesterford, on the London–Cambridge line, to Six Mile Bottom, 8 miles east of Cambridge, thus completely avoiding Cambridge, to which there would only be a branch. The branch was eventually built and the Chesterford–Six Mile Bottom line was closed, having no useful purpose. This is Dullingham, the only passing place on the 16 miles between Cambridge and Chippenham Junction, where the line from Ely is met. The signal box and crossing gates remain. 9 December 1994.

No. 150229 arrives at Kennett with a service from Ipswich. The signal box has been abolished. These multiple units are no longer used in East Anglia. 13 April 1995.

The rather tall station building at Thurston, completed in 1846, was necessitated by the fact that the platforms are on an embankment. This Jacobean style building is no longer in railway use and has listed status. 17 April 1992.

Ely to Norwich

In July 1845 the ECR completed its line from Cambridge to Brandon. On the same day the Norwich & Brandon Railway opened its line from Norwich to Brandon, having by this time merged with the Norwich & Yarmouth Railway to form the Norfolk Railway. A Class 156 unit approaches Brandon with the 16.58 Norwich–Peterborough. The track in the foreground leads to the goods yard, which was reinstated in 1986 for timber traffic. This traffic ceased in 1991. 15 April 1992.

Unit No. 158844 passes Thetford signal box with a service for Norwich. Thetford and Brandon signal boxes, along with all others along the Breckland line, have been abolished. Thetford is a GER type 4 box, containing a McKenzie & Holland frame, and is a listed structure. The line is controlled by Cambridge power box. 13 April 1995.

A classic BR Blue image as No. 37039 passes Wymondham South Junction hauling a rake of Mk 1 coaches, forming the 09.10 Leeds–Yarmouth service. Before its abolition, Wymondham box was the oldest GER signal box still working, having been built in 1877. The resignalling took place in 2012, giving Wymondham South a working life of some 135 years. The line to the left is to Dereham. 30 August 1980.

A sad relic of a time when Wymondham was an important junction. The line to Forncett was opened by the GER in 1881. Passenger traffic ceased at the outbreak of the Second World War, while freight continued only until 1951. The track was lifted in 1952. 17 April 1990.

Ipswich and the Felixstowe and East Suffolk Lines

On 21 August 1980, No. 47117 stands at Ipswich with the 10.32 Norwich to Liverpool Street.

No. 47162 enters the station with a container train from Felixstowe. Notice the white roof, which is typical of Stratford's machines. Notice also the semaphore signals. Ipswich was re-signalled and electrified by 1985. 21 August 1980.

The loop at Derby Road is the only passing place on the 13-mile Felixstowe branch. The Class 101 Metro-Cammell unit, in fact destined for Ipswich, despite the misleading display, surrenders the single line token to the signalman, while No. 37107 waits for the road with a train of containers. These scenes are no more. The signal box has been abolished and the line is now controlled from Colchester. The doubling of the line is planned for the near future. 16 April 1992.

The Westerfield–Felixstowe line was built by the Felixstowe Railway & Pier Company in 1877 and, somewhat remarkably, their original terminal station at Westerfield was still extant in 1992.

The East Suffolk line originated with the Halesworth, Beccles & Haddiscoe Railway, which opened in 1854. In 1859 it was met by the Eastern Union Railway that extended northwards from Woodbridge. The line came close to closure in the 1960s but was saved, largely by a campaign by the East Suffolk Travellers Association. The line was partly singled in the 1960s, with further singling taking place later and leaving double track only between Saxmundham and Halesworth. At one time a large number of services ran through to London. The last of these ran in 1984 and today the service is purely local, with trains running hourly between Lowestoft and Ipswich. In 1986 radio electronic tokenless block was put in place, controlled from Saxmundham. Here we see No. 156404 entering the station with the 14.50 Ipswich–Lowestoft. 16 April 1992.

The branch from Saxmundham to Aldeburgh closed to passengers in 1966. The line remains open to a point beyond Leiston to service the nuclear power station at Sizewell. This is the disused station at Leiston. 16 April 1992.

Norwich to Yarmouth and Lowestoft

Brundall is at the junction of the lines to Yarmouth and Lowestoft. The signals seen here are only for the crossing. There is another signal box at the junction. A Metro-Cammell unit departs with the 14.26 Lowestoft to Norwich on 21 August 1980. A large number of this very successful design were allocated to the Eastern Region. They were the last of the first generation DMUs to remain in service, the last being withdrawn in 2003.

The line between Brundall and Yarmouth is single-track. It was opened in 1883 and is 2½ miles shorter than the original route via Reedham. The only passing place is here, at Acle. A Class 105 Cravens unit waits to depart with the 15.25 Yarmouth–Norwich. The Eastern Region also had a large allocation of this class. 16 April 1992.

The Lowestoft Railway & Harbour Company was set up in 1844 to build the 11¼ miles from Reedham to Lowestoft. In 1846 the Norfolk Railway assumed the lease and the railway opened in 1847. From 1848, operation of the line was by the ECR. The lines from Brundall to Yarmouth and Lowestoft are an oasis of traditional signalling, as at Yarmouth, where we see the departure of the 09.05 to Liverpool in the shape of a Class 156. As well as the block posts there are also a number of gate boxes. The area will be resignalled by 2019 at the latest. 16 April 1992

On 21 August 1980, a Class 105 unit waits to depart from Reedham with the 16.14 Yarmouth–Norwich. Notice the addition of a parcels van, a not uncommon occurrence in those days. Brundall to Reedham and the single-track line beyond Reedham Junction is part of the original route of the Yarmouth & Norwich Railway, which was intended to be the first section of a grand east–west route. It was opened on 30 April 1844. There is a curious story about Berney Arms, the only intermediate station on the single-track section. It was built as a condition of the local landowner allowing the railway to cross his land. He stipulated that the station should remain open in perpetuity; however, he forgot to specify that trains should stop there, and in 1850 the ECR did in fact stop trains calling there. The matter was eventually resolved and trains started calling again. Closure was again proposed in 1985 but the line was reprieved.

There are four railway swing bridges in Norfolk. This is Reedham swing bridge

This is Somerleyton swing bridge; the other swing bridges are at Trowse and Oulton Broad. A Class 101 unit approaches Somerleyton station with a service for Lowestoft.

The same train stands at the platform. The grandeur of the station is accounted for by the fact that this was the home station of Sir Samuel Moreton Peto, chairman of the company that built the line. He inhabited Somerleyton Hall. Curiously, the station building never seems to have had a canopy. Notice also the survival of the BR(ER) blue running-in board. 16 April 1992.

North Norfolk

A Class 101 unit arrives at the delightful station of Salhouse, on the line to Cromer, in order to pick up a solitary passenger. The line is double-track to a point beyond Hoveton and Wroxham and single-track beyond. 17 April 1990.

Above: The driver of a Norwich–Sheringham service has dropped off the single line token, which the signalman is on his way to collect. Since these photographs were taken on 17 April 1990, North Walsham box has been abolished and the line is now controlled by Trowse Swing Bridge.

Left: Sloley Church Lane was one of many manually operated level crossings in Norfolk. It has now been converted to automatic half barriers.

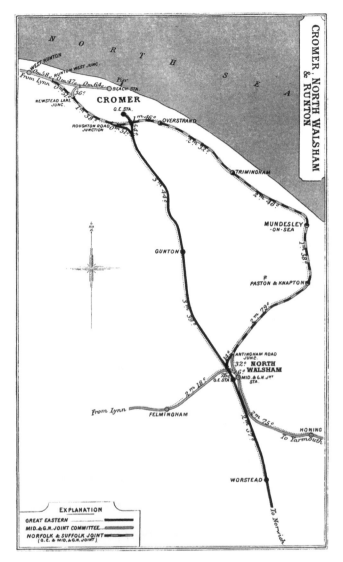

The story of the railways in north-east Norfolk is a complicated one, as might be deduced from the map. First to arrive was the East Norfolk Railway (later Great Eastern), which reached North Walsham in 1874 and Cromer in 1877. At the end of the century the line to North Walsham was doubled but onwards to Cromer it was always single-track. Wroxham to North Walsham was again singled in 1967. The Eastern and Midlands railway opened its line to North Walsham in 1883 and to Cromer in 1887. In 1893 this became the Midland & Great Northern Joint. In 1898 the Great Eastern and the M&GN formed the Norfolk & Suffolk Joint Committee, which built the line from North Walsham to Mundesley and extended it to Cromer in 1906, thus giving the GER access to Cromer for the first time. This line closed north of Mundesley in 1957 and south in 1964. The GER station at Cromer (High) was closed in 1954 and thereafter all services went to the M&GN station (Beach, now just Cromer). Thus it is today that trains to Cromer pass over the former metals of first the GER, then the N&SJt and then the M&GN. The line from Cromer to Sheringham is the only surviving section of the M&GN that is still part of the national network. In addition, there is the North Norfolk Railway. Cromer was a popular holiday destination. The Norfolk Coast Express was a twelve-coach train, which before the First World War completed the journey from London in three hours.

The signal box at Cromer, which is a listed building. At the time of its closure, this was the last working M&GN signal box. As has been mentioned above, the line is now controlled from Trowse Swing Bridge. 18 April 1990.

Essex Branches

A Class 312 EMU stands at Cressing with a service for Braintree on 10 April 1992. The Class 312 was introduced in the mid-1970s to operate Great Northern and Great Eastern outer suburban services. This particular unit ended its days on the London, Tilbury & Southend line. All members of the class were withdrawn by 2004.

The Maldon, Witham & Braintree Railway was authorised in 1846. Before completion it was taken over by the ECR and opened in August 1848. The extension from Braintree to Bishops Stortford followed in 1869. This section lost its passenger services as early as 1952, being closed progressively to freight between 1966 and 1972. Witham to Braintree survived and was electrified in 1977, while Witham to Maldon closed to passengers in 1964 and to freight in 1966. Maldon East station is a listed building.

A Class 321 EMU approaches Wickford with a train from the Southminster branch. It will continue to London.

The 16½-mile Southminster branch was a late addition to the GER network, opening in 1889. A likely candidate for the Beeching axe, it survived after the electrification of the line to Southend, which boosted passenger numbers. It was itself electrified in 1989. This is the pretty terminal station of Southminster. 10 October 1992.

East Midlands

The Midland Main Line

The Midland Counties Railway opened the line from Nottingham to Derby in June 1839, with Trent Junction to Leicester opening in May the following year. No. 46011 stands at Derby with the 12.18 Taunton to Newcastle on 23 November 1981. The Class 46s differed from the more numerous Class 45s in having a main generator supplied by Brush, rather than by Crompton-Parkinson, as fitted to the Class 45s.

In July 1988, at Nottingham Low Level, stands the last ever newspaper train to serve the city. It is 5 a.m. and No. 47417 will shortly depart with the empty stock. All transport of newspapers by train finished the same year. (Photograph Chris Gwilliam)

Four years later the rails have been removed and the station stands derelict and empty. On the extreme left a unit can be seen passing on the Midland Main Line.

Nottingham Low Level (or London Road) was actually the Nottingham station of the GNR. It saw its last passenger trains in 1944 but continued as a parcels station. Today the Grade II listed building is used as a fitness centre.

The surviving station at Nottingham is the Midland station. In this view, taken in February 1993, trains are waiting to leave for Liverpool and Crewe. (Photograph Chris Gwilliam)

Just east of Beeston station, No. 31546 and No. 31178 move from the Up goods to the Up main. In the left background are the Beeston signalling works. The Class 31 was one of the more successful diesel locomotives of the modernisation scheme, although not initially. The locomotives were fitted with the Mirrlees, Bickerton & Day JVS12T engine, giving 1,365 hp. Several machines were fitted with an engine uprated to 1,600 hp and one to 2,000 hp. The original pilot scheme locomotives had been fitted with an engine rated at 1,250 hp, and it was the various upratings that proved to be the downfall of the class, as fatigue fractures started to occur after about five years in service. Rather than carry out repairs BR decided to re-engine the whole class with a downrated version of the English Electric 12SVT, giving 1,470 hp. This proved to be a wise move, leading to an extremely reliable and long-lived machine.

Above and below: It was the North Midland Railway that completed the line from Derby to Chesterfield, with the line opening in July 1840. On 10 May 1844, the NMR, the MCR and the Birmingham & Derby Junction Railway merged to form the Midland Railway. These two photographs show two of the earliest, and most successful, of the diesel-electric types produced under the 1955 Modernisation Plan. On 18 September 1981, near Tapton Junction, just north of Chesterfield, No. 40082 with a train of 21-ton coal hoppers switches from the Down main to the Down goods in order to proceed towards Barrow Hill. At the same location, but this time in 1987, a pair of Class 20s, with No. 20064 leading and newly outshopped in green livery, head north with a train of steel empties.

The original access to London for MR trains was via the MCR Leicester–Rugby line and thence via the London & Birmingham Railway. Congestion at Rugby led the MR to build a line from Leicester to Hitchin via Kettering, Wellingborough and Bedford, and thence to London via the GNR. This is a view of the yard at Bedford. The line to Hitchin would have passed this way, and the main line can be seen in the background. Here we see No. 47975 with a research train waiting for the road through the yard, as a Class 108 DMU leaves with the 12.40 Bedford to Bletchley. 9 March 1992

Finally, the MR completed its own independent route from Bedford to St Pancras in 1868. This section of line was electrified in 1983. Work is in progress at Flitwick on 7 September 1980 with Nos 25324 and 25326 in charge of the electrification trains.

Just north of Ampthill tunnel a Class 127 heads past with a Bedford–St Pancras service. 31 August 1980.

In 1879 the MR opened a line from Kettering to Nottingham via Corby and Old Dalby. Between Manton and Melton Mowbray this used the previously opened Syston and Peterborough line. Corby lost its passenger service in 1967, regained a shuttle service in 1987, lost it in 1990 and finally gained an hourly service to London in 2009. Electrification is planned to be extended from Bedford to Corby by 2019 while Kettering to Derby/Nottingham/Sheffield is scheduled for 2023. In this view we see the diverted 12.00 St Pancras–Sheffield passing through Corby on 18 February 1995.

The branch from Little Eaton to Ripley opened in 1856. Passenger services ended in 1930 but the line remained open for freight traffic. On 7 July 1993, No. 56018 passes over Little Eaton level crossing with a train of coal from the Denby disposal point. Freight traffic ceased in 1999 and the track was lifted in 2012.

Leicester to Peterborough

The Syston & Peterborough Railway completed its lines from Syston Junction to Melton Mowbray and Stamford to Peterborough in October 1846. The Melton–Stamford section was delayed by Lord Harborough, who objected to the railway crossing his land, and it did not open until May 1848. His lordship's objections resulted in the sharply angled 'Lord Harborough's curve' at Saxby. Saxby became a junction in 1898 with the opening of the M&GN line. Before this, Lord Harborough's curve was eased and a new Saxby station built. The new station was closed and abandoned in 1961, although the buildings were not demolished until 2014.

Above: Langham Junction. There is no junction as such here but it is the beginning of a four-track section that reaches to Oakham. The subsidiary signal controls access to the Up goods line. On 20 June 1991, No. 47332 heads south with a train of ballast. Langham signal box, along with the others on this line, is due to be abolished in 2017.

Left: Lampman Bill Causer changes the paraffin signal lamps at Langham – a job he does every seven days.

At Oakham, No. 156412 departs with a service for Harwich. Oakham Level Crossing is a Midland Railway type 2b box dating from about 1900. It is a listed structure. 17 July 1989.

No. 156410 with the 15.04 Norwich to Liverpool Lime Street passes the Ketton Down starter. This signal, which is about 100 years old, is a remarkable survivor; it is the last working Midland Railway lower-quadrant signal on the national network. The continued existence of this museum piece is all the more remarkable as the rest of the semaphore signals at Ketton were replaced by colour lights as long ago as 1989. The signal stands on the outside of the curve rather than to the left of the westbound track so that it can be seen more easily from afar on a curving stretch of line. The signal will disappear when the line is resignalled in 2017. 20 June 1991.

The Erewash Valley Line

No. 56005 comes off the Bennerley branch on to the main line with a loaded MGR. Bennerley loading point was situated on a surviving remnant of the Bennerley & Bulwell Railway, which lost its passenger service as early as 1917. The loading point is now closed and the branch has been disconnected from the main line. 7 July 1993.

Just to the south of the Bennerley branch is the 1,452-foot-long wrought-iron Bennerley Viaduct, which is part of the GNR's Derbyshire extension. Constructed in 1877, it went out of use when the line closed in 1964. It is now a listed structure and due to become part of the national cycle network.

At Trowell, Nos 20078 and 20163 head past with a train of ballast. 29 June 1991.

At Stanton Gate, No. 58014 heads past a line of redundant Class 20s with a loaded MGR. Stanton Gate station closed in 1967 along with others on the Erewash Valley line. The sidings in the foreground have since been removed.

Nos 20010 and 20082 head through Toton Yard with a northbound MGR train. 29 June 1992.

It is clear from this photograph that the main traffic at Toton Yard was coal. Opened in 1856, the yard grew so that in the 1950s 1 million wagons a year were being handled. The collapse of coal traffic has led to much of the yard being closed and the remainder used for stabling wagons and locomotives. Toton Yard is the favoured site for the location of the Midland hub station of the new HS2 high-speed line.

The Robin Hood Line and the South Yorkshire Joint Line

Pinxton is on the freight-only line that links Codnor Park Junction with Kirkby-in-Ashfield. The station of Pinxton and Selston opened with the railway in 1848 and closed ninety-nine years later. Pinxton signal box closed in 2007 after 110 years of service. It has been preserved at Barrow Hill. No. 58030, at the head of an empty MGR train, sets off after a signal check. Note that fixed to the Up starter signal (on the left) is a colour light signal. This is the Sleights East distant, which shows amber when the Pinxton home is pulled off and green when Sleights home is pulled off. 27 July 1991.

The railway reached Mansfield in 1849 and was extended to Worksop in 1875. Mansfield had a passenger service to Nottingham until 1964, after which it became infamous as the largest town in Britain without a passenger station. It regained its passenger status in 1995 with the opening of the Robin Hood Line. Passenger services were extended northwards to Worksop in 1998. This photograph shows No. 58012 heading north through the site of the Mansfield Coal Concentration sidings with an empty MGR train. These sidings went out of use in the 1980s. 13 March 1993.

North of Mansfield is Shirebrook Junction. The Lancashire, Derbyshire & East Coast Railway built its line from Chesterfield to Lincoln in 1897 and it was purchased by the GCR in 1907. The line east of Shirebrook was always primarily a coal line and the somewhat sparse passenger service was withdrawn in 1955. The locomotive passing the signal box is No. 56016. There is now a station at Shirebrook. 17 February 1992.

The line east of Shirebrook remained open for freight, almost exclusively coal traffic. East of Shirebrook is Welbeck Colliery Junction. In a busy scene at the junction, No. 56020 heads towards Shirebrook with a train of empties. Another Class 56 is in the process of running round its train on the branch. Once it departs, No. 58037, which is waiting at the signal, will draw forward and reverse on to the branch. Sadly, such scenes are but just a memory as all the collieries are now closed; however, the line remains in place and there have been discussions about reinstating a passenger service. 1 October 1992.

North of Shirebrook is Elmton & Creswell Junction. Heading south is No. 56003 with an empty MGR train. The signal box is now permanently switched out. This is another location which has gained a railway station. 13 March 1993.

The branch line passing behind the signal box at Elmton and Cresswell led to Seymour Junction. From Seymour Junction a line led to various collieries and to the Bolsover Coalite works, seen here. The works opened in 1937 and closed in 2004. There are no longer any railways in this area. 17 February 1992.

The South Yorkshire Joint Line, which extends the 21.5 miles from Brancliffe East Junction to Kirk Sandall Junction, was built by no less than five different railway companies. Opening in 1909, it was built to serve a number of collieries in the area but also had a passenger service which survived only until 1929. Seen near Firbeck Junction, No. 58012 heads towards Harworth Colliery with a train of empties.

The 'Poacher' Line

Above left: The line from Firsby to Boston was opened in 1848 by the East Lincolnshire Railway, with Grantham to Boston following in 1855. In 1873 the Wainfleet & Firsby and the Wainfleet & Skegness railways completed their sections of track to finally give a through line to Skegness. A Class 101 DMU passes Wainfleet's Down distant with the 11.11 Doncaster to Skegness on 1 July 1991.

Above right: A close up of one of the GNR somersault signals at Wainfleet in the off position. This type of signal arm was introduced after the Abbots Ripton accident, when a signal jammed in the off position.

Below: Sadly, all the GNR somersault signals have been removed. The sole surviving example of this type is at Boston, where this unusual octagonal signal box controls access to the swing bridge leading into the docks.

Boston station on 15 July 1989. No. 31285 arrives with a service for Skegness. The photograph clearly shows that there were once two through lines, which have long since been removed. Since this photograph was taken there have been many more changes, including the replacement of the footbridge and the demolition of all the buildings on the left-hand (Up) platform.

The Jolly Fisherman is a famous poster used to advertise the resort of Skegness. It was also used as the name of steam train excursions from Grantham to Skegness. The train is seen on 10 April 1993 at Heckington on its way to Skegness. The rather attractive signal box at Heckington is a GNR type 1 dating from 1876. Unsurprisingly, it is a listed building.

Skegness on a summer Sunday in 1980. At that time there was still considerable excursion traffic. Lined up and ready to depart are, from left to right: Nos 31115, 45116, 45049, 45018, and 20113. 24 August 1980.

The Great Grimsby & Sheffield Junction Line

Above: The line from Barnetby to Lincoln was completed in 1849. Of the ten original stations along this line only Market Rasen remains open. There was never a station at Stainton, only a level crossing box, which has now gone, being replaced by automatic barriers. On 6 September 1989 a Class 150 DMU heads over the crossing with a Grimsby–Newark service.

Left: Two years later, another Grimsby–Newark train approaches Lincoln station. The train on the left is waiting to cross over to the Up line in order to change platforms at Lincoln station. This kind of manoeuvre is no longer necessary since the platforms at Lincoln have now been signalled for reversible running. 1 July 1991.

The Great Northern & Great Eastern Joint Line

Right: For a long time the GER had wished to penetrate GNR territory, not least to participate in the lucrative Yorkshire coal traffic. Finally, an agreement was reached in 1879 to operate a joint line from Huntingdon to Doncaster via March and Lincoln. The new joint line incorporated sections of railway that had already been built. These were: Huntingdon to March built by the ECR/EAR in 1847/51; the GNR lines from Spalding to March (1867); Pyewipe Junction to Gainsborough (1849); and Gainsborough to Doncaster (1867). The new section of railway needed to complete the line, which stretched from Spalding to Pyewipe Junction, was opened on August 1882, at which time the joint committee took over the management of the line. Of the original thirty-three stations on the joint line, just seven remain open. There were also numerous signal boxes; in 1988 there were still twenty but today just three control the line.

Below: The location of Guyhirne station. Little of the station remains, but the goods shed can be seen in the distance and a lone signal remains in the 'on' position. The photograph was taken from the bridge that carried the railway over the River Nene. The section of line between March and Spalding closed in 1982 but Huntingdon to March had closed by 1970. 12 April 1995.

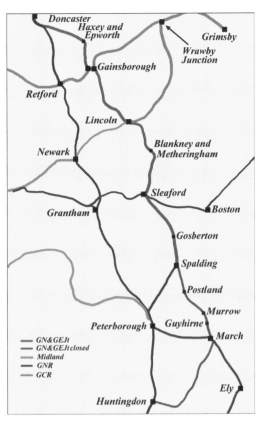

Murrow signal box controlled the flat crossing of the M&GNJt and the GN&GEJt lines. The box dates from 1950 and replaced an earlier structure destroyed by a runaway train. It has recently been converted into a house. 18 April 1990.

The much-diminished station of Spalding, seen here from the south end of Platform 4 in 1989. Spalding first appeared on the railway map in 1848 when the GNR opened its Peterborough–Doncaster main line, which passed through Spalding.

Right: As can be seen from this Railway Clearing House diagram, Spalding was once an important junction, with lines to March, Peterborough, Bourne, Sleaford, Boston and King's Lynn. Today just the Peterborough and Spalding lines remain.

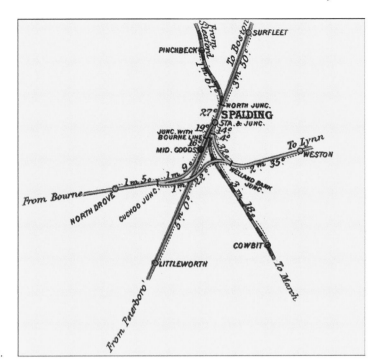

Below: To the south of Spalding, on the line to Peterborough, is Littleworth. The station here closed in 1961 but the signal box was retained until 2013. Before that the crossing gates had been replaced by barriers. On 20 June 1991 a Derby Lightweight unit, resplendent in green livery, passes over the level crossing with the 15.31 Sheffield to Peterborough.

On 20 June 1991, No. 47332 approaches Gosberton crossing with a short engineer's train. The crossing was some distance away from the signal box, which can be seen in the background, and had to be manned with its own cabin. Gosberton station closed in 1961, and since this photograph was taken the signal box has been closed and demolished, with the crossing having been converted to automatic barriers.

On the same day a Class 101 arrives, passing Sleaford East signal box with a Skegness–Doncaster service. The signal box, which dates from 1882 and is a listed structure, is still operational.

A peculiar arrangement existed at Sleaford. The GN&GTJt line passed over the Grantham–Boston line but only freight trains used this line. Passenger trains had to take the curve into the station at Sleaford East and then turn back through a semi-circle to regain the joint line at Sleaford North Junction.

A Class 153 unit, having made its call at Sleaford, heads towards Sleaford North Junction in order to continue its journey to Lincoln. 23 June 1995.

A view of Metheringham station, with the oddly named Blankney signal box. Metheringham station closed in 1961 but was reopened in 1975, along with Ruskington. The signal box is unusual in that it is a GNR type 4 but was built by the LNER in 1928. It is a rare type and for that reason it is listed. In 2014 it was abolished and the crossing gates were replaced by barriers. 19 July 1989.

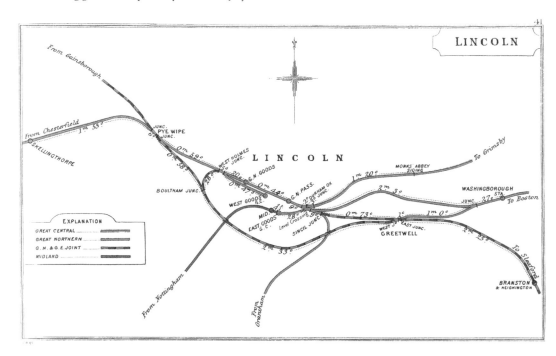

Lincoln is another location with a strange arrangement of lines, including a GN&GEJt avoiding line. This line closed in 1985.

West Holmes Yard, Lincoln, where the joint line had a connection into the GN line in order to access the GN goods depot. The signal box is East Holmes, which is a GN type 1 dating from 1873. It retains its original McKenzie & Holland frame and is a listed building. The box at East Holmes, along with the other signal boxes at Lincoln, was abolished in 2007/8 and replaced by Lincoln Signalling Control Centre. On the right is the GN loco shed. 1 July 1991.

Gainsborough Lea Road is the joint station. The other station, Gainsborough Central, is on the Sheffield–Grimsby line. Neither has a very frequent service. The signal box shown here dates from 1877 and it was closed in 2014.

Haxey and Epworth station closed to passengers in 1959 and to goods in 1964. Between the delightfully named station of Park Drain and Haxey was a connection with the Axholm Light Railway, whose stations of Haxey and Epworth were considerably nearer their respective communities than the joint line station. The Axholm line closed in the 1960s. On 19 August 1989 a Class 101 DMU passes the goods shed at Haxey with a Doncaster–Sleaford service.

Sheffield to Grimsby and South Humberside

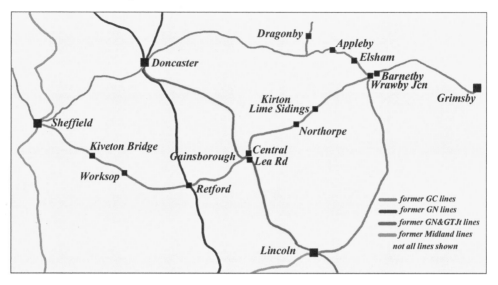

The Manchester, Sheffield & Lincolnshire Railway was formed in 1847 by the amalgamation of a number of separate companies. The opening of the railway between Gainsborough & Woodhouse Junction completed the construction of the MSL's line from Manchester to the East Coast.

On 13 March 1993, single car unit No. 153376 approaches Kiveton Bridge station with the 14.40 Lincoln to Sheffield. The station was opened in 1929 by the LNER after complaints that Kiveton Park station was too far away from the centre of the community. In the background is Kiveton Park colliery, which was still active at the time this photograph was taken but closed the following year.

No. 56020 approaches Worksop station with an eastbound MGR. The subsidiary signals seen on the left are for the Down reception sidings. These signals are no more, as both manual signal boxes at Worksop have been replaced by the new Worksop power signal box. 20 April 1991.

A Class 150 approaches Retford station with a westbound service. While the station is named Retford, the signal box seen in the background is rather curiously named Thrumpton. It has now been replaced with a new box.

Gainsborough Central has a very sparse service indeed which comprised just three return services on Saturdays only. Here we see Pacer No. 142080 with the SO Cleethorpes to Huddersfield.

Northorpe station closed as long ago as 1955. The signal box was retained to control the section and supervise the crossing. It finally closed in 2016. On 19 August 1989 a Class 110 unit passes over the crossing with the SO 14.29 Cleethorpes–Sheffield.

Kirton Lime Sidings signal box was built by the Railway Signal Company for the MSL in 1886. Abolished in 2016, it remains as a listed structure. No. 47224 passes by with a train of tanks bound for Immingham. In the background is the branch into the quarry, which, while still active at this time, is now long since out of use. 19 August 1989.

The magnificent array of signals at Wrawby Junction. The three gantries are for the Down goods, the Down slow and the Down fast. The left-hand signal of each is for the Lincoln line, the centre for the Gainsborough line and the right-hand one for the Scunthorpe line. A Class 150 passes with the 08.58 Newark Northgate to Cleethorpes. The locomotive parked in the siding is No. 20096. Wrawby signal box is in the background. 6 September 1989.

No. 37075 with its short train of tanks is on the Down fast line. The signal is pulled off for the Scunthorpe line. This engine has been preserved and is to be found at the Keighley & Worth Valley Railway. 5 September 1989.

Heading away from the junction on the Lincoln line is No. 150120 with the 12.50 Cleethorpes to Newark Northgate. Wrawby signal box was built in 1916 with a 132-lever frame, to which five were added later. It was the largest manual box worked by one signaller. It closed on Christmas Eve 2015 and the area is now controlled by York Railway Operating Centre. The box remains as a listed building but the semaphore signals are no more. 5 September 1989.

The magnificent Jacobean-style Brocklesby station, disused since its closure in 1993. Its splendour is owed to the fact that it was the home station of the Earl of Yarborough, who lived at Brocklesby Hall and was chairman of the MSL at the time of its construction in 1848. Lord Yarborough and his guests had their own private waiting room in the station. It is a Grade II listed building.

Barnetby East is another signal box which closed at the end of 2015 and has now been demolished. No. 153357 heads towards Cleethorpes. 28 June 1993.

Left: A view towards Grimsby station from the east as a Pacer leaves for Cleethorpes. The signal box is Garden Street, an MSL type 2 dating from 1881. It was abolished in 1993 along with the other four signal boxes at Grimsby. The crossing gates have been replaced by barriers. Notice the blast wall around the base of the box, which was built as an air raid precaution.

Below: The Trent, Ancholme & Grimsby Railway was opened in 1866 between Wrawby Junction and Gunness, where it made an end-on connection with the South Yorkshire Railway. It later became part of the MSL. Elsham station closed in October 1993. No. 60003 heads through with a train of iron ore bound for Scunthorpe. 28 June 1993.

The next station after Elsham was Appleby, which closed in 1967. Appleby and Elsham signal boxes were both built by the Railway Signal Company in 1885. Both are listed though they have now been abolished. On 28 June 1990, No. 158756 is in charge of the 13.26 Cleethorpes–Manchester.

In 1906 the North Lindsey Light Railway built a line from Frodingham to West Halton, which was later extended to Whitton. Dragonby sidings are situated on the Flixborough branch, which leaves the NLLR at Normanby Park. On 28 June 1993, RFS Industries No. 1 *Terence* shunts a train of steel bar.

The Hope Valley

The Midland Railway's Hope Valley route was one of the last major lines to be built. Originally proposed by the Dore & Chinley Railway, it was eventually taken over by the MR and was fully operational by June 1894. It includes the two tunnels of Totley (3 miles, 950 yards) and Cowburn (2 metres, 182 yards). Remarkably, all the intermediate stations remain open, not least because of the popularity of the Hope Valley as a destination for ramblers. One of the most popular destinations for walkers is Edale. No. 158782 passes Edale signal box with the 08.54 Liverpool–Norwich. 31 August 1992.

The next signal box east of Edale is Earles Sidings. A Class 124 on a Sheffield–Manchester service unit has been stopped by the signalman to be warned of sheep further up the line. These units were built at Swindon in 1960 specifically for the Trans-Pennine service. In 1984 they were all withdrawn, being replaced by Class 31/4 hauled trains. 15 October 1981.

Earles Sidings was the originating point of an important traffic in cement from the nearby Hope cement works. On 21 April 1981, No. 40139 pulls away from the sidings with a train of Presflo wagons.

The Uttoxeter to Willington Line

The North Staffordshire Railway opened a line from Uttoxeter to Burton-on-Trent in September 1848. An extension from Marston Junction to North Stafford Junction followed a year later, bringing the NSR to its furthest point east. At Scropton a Class 108 unit approaches the crossing with the 13.10 Nottingham–Crewe. 28 April 1991.

To the east of Scropton is Tutbury Crossing. The signal box is something of a gem; built by McKenzie & Holland in 1872, it is the only surviving McKenzie & Holland Mk 1 box. It also retains its McKenzie & Holland frame of 1897.

To the north of North Stafford Junction is Stenson Junction, which gives access to the freight-only line to Sheet Stores Junction. On this line on 7 July 1995 is No. 58012 with an empty MGR train. Notice that the locomotive is already carrying the logo of 'Mainline' – one of the three short-lived companies set up immediately prior to privatisation. Later the locomotives of this company would be painted in an all-over blue.

The East Coast Main Line

On 1 June 1980, No. 31222 stands at Peterborough, waiting to leave with a mail train for King's Cross.

The impressive Digswell Viaduct at Welwyn, which was built to carry the ECML over the River Mimram. The viaduct is 475 metres long and took two years to build. The viaduct and the two Welwyn tunnels form something of a bottleneck on the ECML, which otherwise is quadruple-tracked from King's Cross to Huntingdon. From time to time possible solutions are discussed but nothing ever happens. On 6 June 1980 a pair of Class 31s head south with a passenger train.

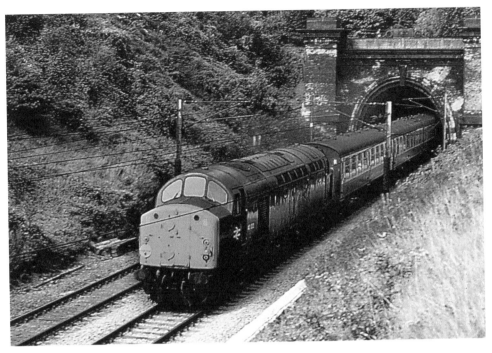

No. 40003 emerges from Welwyn North tunnel with a southbound train. The headcode indicates that this is an empty stock working. 6 September 1980.

Unit No. 313020 has stopped at a signal between the two Welwyn tunnels in order for the driver to report that smoke from stubble burning is obscuring sighting of the signal. This train is also an empty stock working. 6 September 1980.

At the famous flat crossing to the north of Newark Northgate station, No. D6607 *Ben Cruachan*, resplendent in early BR livery, heads east towards Lincoln. The two bridges in the background take the railway across the River Trent. No. D6607 has had a number of identity change; it used to be No. 37403 and before that it was No. 37307. It is now named *Isle of Mull*.

The 'Ivanhoe' Line

The Leicester & Swannington Railway was opened in 1833, primarily as a line to move coal. Robert Stephenson was the engineer. It was purchased by the Midland in 1846 and extended to Burton in 1849. It lost its passenger service in 1964. In the early 1990s plans were in hand to reopen the line to passengers; unfortunately, these plans got overtaken by the chaos of privatisation and were shelved. A recent report has found that the cost of restoring the line to passenger status would be uneconomic and is now unlikely to happen. In June 1988 No. 58032 is seen at Mantle Lane with an MGR train. Although the coal traffic has now disappeared, the line is sustained by the quarries at Bardon Hill and Stud Farm. (Photograph Chris Gwilliam)

The South

The South Eastern Railway

The Medway Valley line was built by the South Eastern Railway in two stages; the first in 1844 from Paddock Wood, on the London–Folkestone/Dover main line, to Maidstone West, and the second from Maidstone to Strood, on the North Kent line, in 1856. In this view we see 4-CEP unit No. 1601 arriving at Cuxton with a service for Paddock Wood. These Eastleigh-built units were introduced in 1956 and were all retired by 2005.

Cuxton no longer has semaphore signals and eventually all signalling on this line will be controlled by the new North Kent Operations Centre. The clapperboard-built Cuxton signal box, seen beyond the bridge, is thought to have been constructed by the South Eastern Railway in about 1888. Little has changed since its construction and it still has a South Eastern 7-foot Brady lever frame. For these reasons it is a listed structure. Notice that the semaphore arm is shorter than usual so that it does not foul the footbridge.

At Snodland, 4-CEP unit No. 1530 stands with the 13.03 Strood to Paddock Wood. Snodland is another station that has lost its semaphores. The Down platform has a wooden canopy attached to a substantial wall, which is in fact the last surviving part of the goods shed that, apart from this wall, was demolished in the 1980s.

At New Hythe a train for Strood approaches the station. At the time of this photograph the siding was still receiving deliveries of coal twice a week. The distant signal seen on the left was worked by Aylesford signal box, a pull of more than 1,500 yards.

The contractor for the Medway line was Edward Betts, through whose estate at Preston Hall the line passed. His local station was Aylesford, hence the reason for its unusual grandeur. At the time this photograph was taken it had just received a £250,000 refurbishment. The SECR signal box at Aylesford is another listed structure.

Unit No. 1601 is seen again, having arrived at Maidstone West with a train from Strood. There is no physical connection between Maidstone West and the London, Chatham & Dover-built Maidstone East. The Medway Valley Line between Strood and Maidstone West was electrified by July 1939 but the remaining section to Paddock Wood had to wait until 1961.

At East Farleigh the signalman reopens the crossing gates as a Paddock Wood–Strood service recedes into the distance. The station buildings, which date from the 1844 opening of the line, are a good example of the South Eastern's Kentish clapperboard style and, apart from the loss of the brick chimneys, are largely original. The 1892 signal box has since been modified and the semaphore signals were replaced by colour lights in 2005.

In 1846 the SER constructed a line from Ashford, where the railway had arrived from London in 1842, via Canterbury to Margate. 4-CEP unit No. 1538 arrives at Wye with the 13.04 Margate to Charing Cross. Notice the beautiful Southern Railway lampshades and concrete lamp posts. These lamp posts, together with many other concrete structures, were made at the Exmouth Junction concrete works. Unfortunately, all have now gone, having been replaced by more 'modern' lights. The signal post is made from two old rails. There are no longer any semaphores at Wye and the signal box has been abolished. 10 April 1990.

At Chartham another clapperboard signal box, following the resignalling of this line in 2003, was reduced to just a gatebox. Chartham did not have a station when the line opened. The residents of the village had had a clause inserted into the authorising act forbidding the construction of a station at Chartham and it wasn't until 1859 that one was eventually built. 10 April 1990.

The simple elegance of Canterbury West reflects the aesthetic of its time, before the fussiness of the later Victorian period took over. The fact that it remains in almost entirely original condition is justification for its listed status.

The SER, much to the chagrin of its neighbour, the LBSCR, built the line from Ashford to just west of Hastings. The LBSCR had opened its line from Lewes in 1846 but had to wait until 1851 for the arrival of the SER from Ashford. The two railways made an end-on connection at Bo Peep Junction, just to the west of Hastings. The chagrin of the London & Brighton was due to the fact that it had wanted to build the line from Ashford. Such was the ill feeling between the two companies that a virtual battle erupted at Hastings when the SER line arrived in February and matters were not resolved until December of that year. Appledore was one of only four intermediate stations on the line. It is also the junction of the freight only line to Dungeness, which has been retained to serve the nuclear power station. This line lost its passenger service in 1967. The signal box seen on the right dates from 1954 and has since been demolished. Note the awning attached to the wall of the goods shed, as at Snodland, though in this case, happily, the goods shed has survived. 10 April 1990.

Hastings

In the following year the SER line from London to Hastings was completed. Seen here is a general view of Hastings station in April 1990. The goods yard, seen in the background, has since been lifted and been built over. In Platform 1 can be seen a train which has arrived on an Ashford–Hastings service. This is 'Hastings' DEMU No. 203001, which survived on this service until later in 1990. Happily, the bracket signals seen in the foreground with their lattice post dolls still survive.

The magnificent 1931 station building at Hastings is magnificent no more, as it has been demolished and replaced with an ultramodern structure. 11 April 1990.

It was apparent as soon as the Hastings line had been completed that there were problems with its construction. The tunnels had been lined with only four courses of brick, which was insufficient. The addition of two further courses made the tunnels too narrow for ordinary rolling stock. As a result, special stock had to be built to be able to pass through the tunnels safely. On 21 September 1948, Schools Class 4-4-0 No. 30936 *Cranleigh* waits to depart with a service to Hastings. Note the flat-sided stock, which was built specially for the Hastings line. The Schools Class of locomotives were also built to fit the Hastings line loading gauge. (Photograph Ben Brooksbank)

After the withdrawal of steam traction the Hastings DEMUs – Classes 201–203 – were introduced on the line. In 1986 the line was electrified and the track singled through the narrow tunnels, thus allowing the use of normal gauge rolling stock. In that final year of service Unit No. 1601 waits to leave Hastings with a service for London. Notice that the third rail is already in place. (Photograph Lamberhurst)

London, Brighton & South Coast Railway

The LBSCR developed lines along the coast both east and west of its Brighton terminus. The line from Lewes to St Leonards was opened in 1846. Pevensey & Westham suffered several name changes before settling down to its present one in 1890. The line was electrified in 1935. The signal box is of interest; it is a Saxby & Farmer type 5 dating from 1876 and was abolished in 2015. On 11 April 1990, a 4-CIG unit arrives at the station with a Brighton–Ore service.

The platform ends at Littlehampton in April 1990, with a unit waiting to leave for London. The semaphore signals seen here survive but sadly the lattice-post dolls have been replaced by standard BR dolls. The LBSCR opened the west coast line in stages between 1845 and 1847, reaching Portsmouth on 14 June 1847. The original Littlehampton station was on the main line. This closed in 1863 when the 2½-mile branch to the present station was opened.

The view from the country end of Littlehampton. The signal box is a LBSCR type 2, dating from 1886. The valancing under the roof is very unusual for signal boxes and it is this feature and the fact the box retains its 1901 LBSCR Bosham-pattern frame that cause it to be a listed building.

Holmwood, on the Mid-Sussex line. 4EPB unit No. 5416 leaves with a Victoria–Horsham service. Although built by British Railways, the 5400 series of EPB units was a Southern Railway design. The last units were withdrawn in 1995.

Holmwood signal box is a Saxby & Farmer type 5, which was constructed about 1876. It has its original Saxby & Farmer frame, and is a listed structure, though no longer operational. It is now heavily protected against vandalism but when this photograph was taken in April 1990 the key to the signal box lay on a stone just to the rear of the signal box door!

Billingshurst, another station on the Mid-Sussex line, looking remarkably original and complete. When this photograph was taken on 11 April 1990, the signal box was still active and was the oldest signal box in Britain still in use. It is a Saxby & Farmer type 1b and is thought to have been constructed in 1868. The box was abolished in 2014 and removed to Amberley Chalk Pits Museum.

Further south on the Mid-Sussex is Amberley. The Mid-Sussex was built as a response by the LBSCR to the LSWR's new London–Portsmouth 'direct' line, which was a shorter route than the LBSCR route via the 'West Coast'. The Mid-Sussex shortened the LBSCR route to Portsmouth by 8 miles. The small grey structure on the platform is the signal box. It was abolished in 2014.

Cosham Junction was where the LBSCR met the LSWR. From there to Portsmouth the two companies agreed to build a joint line. At Fratton there was a branch to Southsea opened in 1885 but it was not a success and the line closed completely in 1914. 4-CIG unit No. 1309 passes the yard at Fratton with the 08.38 Eastleigh to Portsmouth Harbour. Introduced in 1964, the last of these units was withdrawn in 2005. 23 April 1992.

In 1845 the GWR was authorised to build the Berks & Hants Railway, which consisted of a branch from Reading to Hungerford and another to Basingstoke. The Basingstoke line, which was broad gauge, opened in 1848. A third rail was laid in 1856 to allow the passage of standard-gauge trains. Broad-gauge trains stopped using the line in 1869. Bramley gained a goods siding in 1865 but did not become a passenger station until 1895. A Class 207 departs with a service for Basingstoke. 25 April 1992.

London & South Western Railway

Micheldever station presents a simple but harmonious elegance. Designed by Sir William Tite, its largely original condition has led to it becoming a listed building. Interestingly, the adjacent telephone box is also listed. Micheldever, originally Andover Road, opened with the completion of the London–Southampton route by the London & South Western Railway in 1840. The line was electrified in 1967.

A pair of Class 205 'Thumpers' cross at Andover. The 66 headcode indicates that this is a Reading–Yeovil service. The Class 205 units were built at Eastleigh between 1957 and 1962. Originally designated 2H, they became 3H when a centre car was added, and later Class 205. They were equipped with the English Electric 61 litre 4SRKT Mk 2 engine of 600 bhp. The last of these units was withdrawn in 2004. The railway reached Andover from Basingstoke in 1854 and was extended to Salisbury in 1857. The line on the left leads to the Ludgershall branch, which is currently used by the MOD. Go-Op, an open access operator, plans to operate a light rail passenger service on this branch. 25 April 1992.

A view of Salisbury station from the west. A line of redundant Class 33 locomotives is claiming the attention of a photographer.

No. 50037 stands at Salisbury, having arrived with the 14.15 Waterloo–Salisbury on 14 July 1990. The Class 50 locomotive was based around the English Electric V16 engine first used in the LMS diesels Nos 10000 and 10001. In those locomotives the engine was rated at 1,600 hp. In the Class 40 the Mk 2 16SVT was rated at 2,000 hp. The engine fitted to the Class 50s was the 16CSVT – the 'C' standing for intercooling – and was now rated at 2,700 hp. This was a massive piece of machinery. The cylinder bore was 254 mm and the stroke 305 mm, giving an engine capacity of 247 litres. The Class 50s ended their service on the Waterloo–Exeter trains in May 1992.

Authorised in 1844, it was to be another three years before the line between Eastleigh and Salisbury came into use. Once it did so it became the route for trains from Salisbury to London, until the opening of the line to Salisbury from Basingstoke. No. 158827 heads past the branch to East Grimstead Quarry with the 16.20 Portsmouth Harbour to Cardiff. The quarry remains rail connected, though it is long out of use. 28 June 1992.

The Devon Belle, hauled by Bulleid Light Pacific No. 34027 *Taw Valley*, is seen near Romsey. The locomotive is carrying the correct headcode for the Eastleigh–Salisbury line. 28 June 1992.

Southern Railway

The Southern Railway opened the 9-mile Fawley branch in 1925. The main reason for its construction was to service the refinery at Fawley but a number of passenger stations were also built, including here at Marchwood. Passenger services were withdrawn in 1966. Following the cessation of oil traffic to Fawley the line has been mothballed beyond Marchwood, but remains open at that point to service the MOD depot. This view north from the platform shows that on the nearer signals the lattice-work dolls have been retained and fitted to a new bracket. The other set of signals remains in its original condition.

East London

In July 1983 a Class 105 Cravens unit passes over Stratford Southern Junction as it leaves Stratford Low Level with a train for North Woolwich. The lines on the left lead only as far as the civil engineer's depot. The North Woolwich Railway opened in 1847 between North Woolwich and Stratford. The Low Level station was opened when the line was extended northwards.

A view taken in the opposite direction as a Class 116 DMU arrives with a North Woolwich–Stratford service. The rusting tracks on the right lead to Stratford Market Depot. In the background can be seen Stratford Market station. Opened with the line and originally named Stratford Bridge, it was renamed Stratford Market in 1880. It closed in 1957.

This photograph, taken from a point further south, shows a North Woolwich service passing Stratford Market, which is seen on the left. The Market Depot was opened by the GER in 1879 to enable produce to be brought directly into London from the East Anglian farms. It went out of use in the early 1980s. Stratford Market station is seen once again in the background.

In 2010 the scene at Stratford Low Level has totally changed. On the right, where once was the civil engineer's depot, are the platforms of the Jubilee line, and on the left the platforms are being prepared to receive Docklands Light Railway trains. The roof of Stratford Market station can just be glimpsed above the footbridge. (Photograph Ben Brooksbank)

At Liverpool Street station a Class 47 passes through a maze of tracks and overhead lines as it arrives with a service from Norwich. July 1983.

On 27 October 1980, Deltic No. 55009 *Alycidon* stands at King's Cross, having arrived with the 09.33 from Hull. No. 55009 is one of the six Deltics that have been preserved.

The line to Tilbury was opened by the predecessor of the London, Tilbury & Southend Railway in 1854. In 1930 a new station was built and the station was renamed Tilbury Riverside. It was an important disembarkation point for ocean liners. There were four platform lines for passengers and two for baggage. In 1955, 500 liners called and boat trains carried 147,298 passengers to London.

On 27 June 1992, and amid signs of neglect, a Class 312 unit arrives at Tilbury with the 10.36 from Upminster. Train services were withdrawn just five months later.

A Class 115 unit arrives at Leytonstone with a service for Barking. Opened in 1894, the Tottenham & Forest Gate Railway, which linked Tottenham and Woodgrange Park, was a joint line of the Midland Railway and the London & Tilbury. It ceased to be a joint line following the absorption of the latter by the former. From the late nineteenth century onwards, the line was used by boat trains from St Pancras to Tilbury for a period. The line is due to be electrified by 2018. The Class 115 units were built by BR Derby in 1960 and the last were withdrawn in 1998. 27 June 1992.

Temple Mills

The yard at Temple Mills came into use in 1896 when the GER set up a wagon works. In the mid-1950s the yard was modernised as a hump yard – supposedly 'the most modern marshalling yard in Britain'.

The view north from the Ruckholt Road Bridge in September 1989. By now the yard is no longer operational as a marshalling yard; it has been partly lifted and the remainder used for storage. On the left are the electrified Tottenham–Stratford lines.

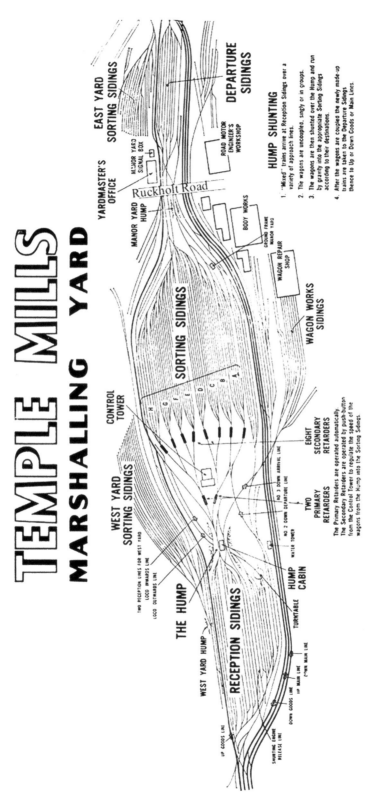

This is the yard as originally laid out in the 1950s.

A view taken from the Hump Cabin towards the Control Tower in 1989.

In happier times, 'Skinhead' No. 31013 arrives at the west end of the yard with a short engineer's train. On the right are the Lea Bridge gas works – a substantial customer of the railway. The works closed with the arrival of North Sea gas. 27 May 1977. (Photograph Peter Groom)

Another view taken from the Ruckholt Road Bridge in 2007 shows a totally transformed scene. This is the Eurostar maintenance depot, which opened that year. (Photograph Ben Brooksbank)

West London

Neasden South Junction. On 30 May 189 a Class 115 unit heads past with an Aylesbury–Marylebone service. Network South East has been in place for three years but so far only two of the carriages of this unit have received the new livery. The tracks to the left are to Princes Risborough while the track adjacent to the signal box leads round to Neasden Junction. Neasden South Junction signal box is something of a curiosity. It is a box of Great Central design, which came into being with the opening of the GCR London Extension. However, the signals that can be seen consist of a GWR bracket signal with standard BR upper quadrant arms!

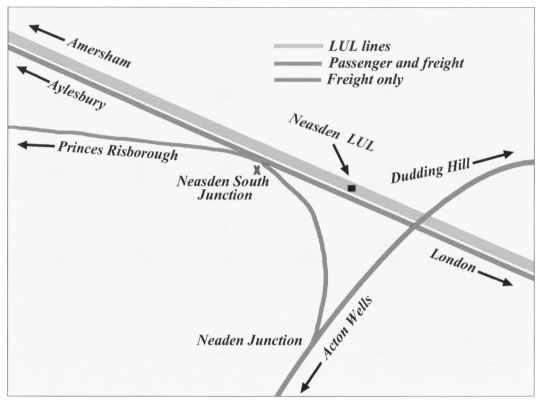

The layout at Neasden South Junction.

No. 47468 is reversing a short train of tanks from Neasden Junction, on the Dudding Hill line, towards Neasden South Junction.

Having completed the manoeuvre and gained the main line, No. 47468 sets off towards London. Notice the typical Great Central signal, with wooden dolls on a lattice post support. Neasden LU station is seen in the background. 30 May 1989.

In May 1985 a Class 501 unit approaches Wembley Central on the DC lines with a Euston–Watford service. The units were withdrawn the same year, after thirty years of service. (Photograph Martin Addison)

In July 1987 2-EPB unit No. 6315 leaves Willesden High Level with a service for North Woolwich. These units were introduced to replace the Class 501 units but were themselves replaced by Class 313 units. (Photograph Martin Addison)

On 23 November 1983, 1A07, the 21.35 sleeper from Penzance to Paddington headed by No. 50041 *Bulwark*, approached the terminus too fast and the locomotive turned over on its side. The carriages remained more or less upright and only three people were injured.